CALL HER BLESSED
(Proverbs 31:28)

A Patchwork for the Woman of Purpose

D1502660

A BARBOUR BOOK

All Scripture quotations are from the King James Version of the Bible unless otherwise noted.

Scripture taken from the HOLY BIBLE, NEW INTERNATIONAL VERSION. Copyright © 1973, 1978, 1984 by International Bible Society.

Published by Barbour and Company, Inc.
            P.O. Box 719
            Uhrichsville, Ohio 44683

Typeset by Typetronix, Inc., Cape Coral, Florida

ISBN 1-55748-271-3

Printed in the United States of America

    2   3   4   5/ 97   96   95   94   93

If instead of a gem, or even a flower, we could cast the gift of a lovely thought into the heart of a friend, that would be giving as the angels give.

George MacDonald

$\mathbb{H}$*er children arise up, and call her blessed; her husband also, and he praiseth her.*

Proverbs 31:28

$\mathbb{D}$*aughter, be of good comfort: thy faith hath made thee whole; go in peace.*

Luke 8:48

There is in every true woman's heart a spark of heavenly fire, which lies dormant in the broad daylight of prosperity, but which kindles up and beams and blazes in the dark hour of adversity.

Washington Irving

*Y*et *in my dreams I'd be
Nearer, my God, to Thee,
Nearer to Thee.*

Sarah Flower Adams

Then took Mary a pound of ointment . . . very costly, and anointed the feet of Jesus, and wiped his feet with her hair: and the house was filled with the odour of the ointment.

John 12:3

$\mathbb{S}$*he considereth a field and buyeth it: with the fruit of her hands she planteth a vineyard. She girdeth her loins with strength, and strengtheneth her arms.*

Proverbs 31:16-17

When we do the best that we can, we never know what miracle is wrought in our life, or in the life of another.

Helen Keller

Women are poets by just
being women.

José Martí

...*My heart rejoiceth in the Lord, mine horn is exalted in the Lord: my mouth is enlarged over mine enemies; because I rejoice in thy salvation.*

HANNAH
1 Samuel 2:1

Awake, *awake, Deborah: awake, awake, utter
a song. . . .*

DEBORAH
Judges 5:31

CALL HER BLESSED

We never know how high we are
Till we are called to rise;
And then, if we are true to plan,
Our statures touch the skies.

Emily Dickinson

$\mathbb{F}$*rom women's eyes this doctrine I derive:*
They sparkle still the right Promethean fire;
They are the books, the arts, the academes,
That show, contain, and nourish all the world.

William Shakespeare

The aged women . . . be in behaviour as becometh holiness, not false accusers, not given to much wine, teachers of good things; that they may teach the young women to be sober, to love their husbands, to love their children.

Titus 2:3-4

$\mathbb{G}$*od hath made me to laugh, so that all that hear will laugh with me.*

SARAH
Genesis 21:6

*There are two ways of spreading light:
to be
The candle or the mirror that reflects it.*

Edith Wharton

T*he happiest women, like the happiest nations, have no history.*

George Eliot
(Marian Evans Cross)

Who can find a virtuous woman? for her price is far above rubies.

Proverbs 31:10

. . . If ye have judged me to be faithful to the Lord, come into my house, and abide there. . . .

LYDIA
Acts 16:15b

I*f the time should ever come when women are not Christians and houses are not homes, then we shall have lost the chief cornerstones on which civilization rests.*

Andrew Dickson White

Such is beauty ever,— neither here nor there, now nor then,— neither in Rome nor in Athens, but wherever there is a soul to admire.

Henry David Thoreau

F*avour is deceitful and beauty is vain: but a woman that feareth the* Lord, *she shall be praised.*

Proverbs 31:30

Great events make me quiet and calm; it is only trifles that irritate my nerves.

Queen Victoria

No coward soul is mine,
No trembler in the world's storm-troubled sphere:
I see Heaven's glories shine,
And faith shines equal, arming me from fear.

Emily Brontë

Ah, tell me not that memory
Sheds gladness o'er the past;
What is recalled by faded flowers
Save that they did not last?
Were it not better to forget,
Than but remember and regret?

Letitia Elizabeth Landon

I*t seems that it is madder never to abandon one's self than often to be infatuated; better to be wounded, a captive and a slave, than always to walk in armor.*

Margaret Fuller

I *am the rose of Sharon, and the lily of the valleys. As the lily among thorns, so is my love among the daughters.*

THE BRIDE
Song of Solomon 2:1-2

Grow old along with me!
The best is yet to be,
The last of life, for which the first was made.
Our times are in His hand.

Robert Browning

Never the time and the place
And the loved one all together!

Robert Browning

CALL HER BLESSED

And Jacob served seven years for Rachel;
and they seemed unto him but a few days, for
the love he had to her.

Genesis 29:20

Fo*r how can I endure to see the evil that shall come unto my people? or how can I endure to see the destruction of my kindred?*

ESTHER
Esther 8:6

The surest way to get a thing done in this
life is to be prepared for doing without it, to
the exclusion even of hope.

Jane Welsh Carlyle

N*o man is poor who has had a Godly mother.*
Abraham Lincoln

CALL HER BLESSED

For whosoever shall do the will of my Father
which is in heaven, the same is my brother, and
sister, and mother.

Matthew 12:50

. . . Intreat me not to leave thee, or to return from following after thee: for whither thou goest, I will go; and where thou lodgest, I will lodge: thy people shall be my people, and thy God my God.

RUTH
Ruth 1:16

CALL HER
BLESSED

N*ecessity can set me helpless on my back,
but she cannot keep me there; nor can
four walls limit my vision.*

"Michael Fairless"
(Margaret Fairless Barber)

Woman, *God bless her by that name, for it is a far nobler name than lady.*

Walter von der Vogelweide

And the LORD God caused a deep sleep to fall upon Adam, and he slept: and he took one of his ribs, and closed up the flesh instead thereof; and the rib, which the LORD God had taken from man, made he woman. . . .

Genesis 2:21-22

I *have been reminded of your sincere faith,
which first lived in your grandmother Lois and
in your mother Eunice and, I am persuaded,
now lives in you also.*

2 Timothy 1:5 (NIV)

CALL HER
BLESSED

$\mathbb{A}$ *rich child often sits in a poor mother's lap.*

Danish proverb

As unto the bow the cord is,
So unto the man is woman;
Though she bends him, she obeys him,
Though she draws him, yet she follows;
Useless each without the other.

H.W. Longfellow

CALL HER
BLESSED

The LORD *hath created a new thing in earth,
a woman shall compass a man.*

Jeremiah 31:22

...I *have drunk neither wine nor strong drink, but have poured out my soul before the* Lord.

HANNAH
1 Samuel 1:15

CALL HER
BLESSED

I *should not dare to call my soul my own.*

Elizabeth Barrett Browning

So many worlds, so much to do,
So little done, such things to be.

Alfred, Lord Tennyson

. . .Martha, Martha, thou art careful and troubled about many things: But one thing is needful: and Mary hath chosen that good part, which shall not be taken away from her.

Luke 10:41-42

49

All the privilege I claim for my own sex ... is that of loving longest, when existence or when hope is gone.

Jane Austen

The greatest love is a mother's; then comes a dog's; then comes a sweetheart's.

Polish proverb

...Sometimes a woman's love of being loved gets the better of her conscience.

Thomas Hardy

CALL HER *BLESSED*

Not a hundredth part of the thoughts in my head have ever been or ever will be spoken or written — as long as I keep my senses, at least.

Jane Welsh Carlyle

I *know that Messias cometh, which is called Christ: when he is come, he will tell us all things.*

THE SAMARITAN WOMAN
John 4:25

CALL HER BLESSED

Be thou my Vision,
O Lord of my heart;
Nought be all else to me,
save that Thou art.

Mary Byrne

I*f you stop to be kind you must swerve often
from your path.*

Mary Webb

CALL HER BLESSED

*S*he opens her arms to the poor and extends
her hands to the needy. When it snows, she has
no fear for her household; for all of them are
clothed in scarlet.

Proverbs 31: 20-21 (NIV)

Sing ye to the LORD, for he hath triumphed gloriously; the horse and his rider hath he thrown into the sea.

MIRIAM
Exodus 15:21

CALL HER *BLESSED*

CALL HER BLESSED

I *could not hope
to touch the sky
with my two arms.*

Sappho
(612 B.C.)

CALL HER
BLESSED

My *old father used to have a saying that*
"If you made a bad bargain, hug it the tighter."

Abraham Lincoln

CALL HER BLESSED

A wife of noble character is her husband's crown, but a disgraceful wife is like decay in his bones.

Proverbs 12:4 (NIV)

A*nd when she could not longer hide him, she took for him an ark of bulrushes, and daubed it with slime and with pitch, and put the child therein; and she laid it in the flags by the river's brink.*

Exodus 2:3

Take love when love is given,
But never think to find it
A sure escape from sorrow
Or a complete repose.

Sara Teasdale

I *do not own an inch of land,*
But all I see is mine.

Lucy Larcom

CALL HER BLESSED

And there came a certain poor widow, and she threw in two mites, which make a farthing. And he . . . saith unto them, . . . For all they did cast in of their abundance; but she of her want did cast in all that she had, even all her living.

Mark 12:42-44

And now, my daughter, fear not; I will do
to thee all that thou requirest: for all the city of
my people doth know that thou art a virtuous
woman.

NAOMI
Ruth 3:11

Woman is woman's natural ally.

Euripides

Women *are never stronger than when they
arm themselves with their weaknesses.*

Madame du Deffand

A *soft answer turneth away wrath.*

Proverbs 15:1

And there was one Anna, a prophetess, . . . which departed not from the temple, but served God with fastings and prayers night and day. And she coming in that instant gave thanks and spake of him to all them that looked for redemption in Jerusalem.

Luke 2:36-38

All the way my Saviour leads me;
What have I to ask beside?
Can I doubt His tender mercy,
Who through life has been my Guide?

Fanny Crosby

We *grow old as soon as we cease to love and trust.*

Madame de Choiseul

CALL HER
BLESSED

$\mathbb{M}$*oreover, his mother [Hannah] made him a little coat and brought it to him from year to year when she came with her husband to offer the yearly sacrifice.*

1 Samuel 2:19

S*he never quite leaves her children at home,
even when she doesn't take them along.*

Margaret Culkin Banning

CALL HER BLESSED

Who ran to help me when I fell,
And would some pretty story tell,
Or kiss the place to make it well?
My mother.

Ann Taylor
(1804)

Marriage, *to women as to men, must be a luxury, not a necessity; an incident of life, not all of it.*

Susan Brownell Anthony

To *know the right woman is a liberal education.*

Elbert Hubbard

And it came to pass, that, when Elisabeth
heard the salutation of Mary, the babe leaped
in her womb; and Elisabeth was filled with the
Holy Ghost.

Luke 1:41

$\mathbb{A}$ *mother is not a person to lean on, but a person to make leaning unnecessary.*

Dorothy Canfield Fisher

W*hen a woman ceases to alter the fashion of her hair, you guess that she has passed the crisis of her experience.*

Mary Austin

CALL HER
BLESSED

If *a woman have long hair, it is a glory to her.*

1 Corinthians 11:15

E*very wise woman buildeth her house: but
the foolish plucketh it down with her hands.*

Proverbs 14:1

I *do not ask for any crown*
But that which all may win;
Nor try to conquer any world
Except the one within.

Louisa May Alcott

If a woman had no existence save in the fiction written by men, one would imagine her a person of the utmost importance; very various; heroic and mean; splendid and sordid; infinitely beautiful and hideous in the extreme; as great as a man, some think even greater.

Virginia Woolf

The woman who is known only through a man is known wrong.

Henry Adams

My soul doth magnify the Lord, and my
spirit hath rejoiced in God my Saviour. For he
hath regarded the low estate of his handmaiden:
for, behold, from henceforth all generations shall
call me blessed.

MARY
Luke 1:46-48

CALL HER
BLESSED

O*f all the rights of women, the greatest is to
be a mother.*

Lin Yutang

I *commend unto you Phebe our sister . . .
that ye receive her in the Lord, as becometh
saints . . . for she hath been a succourer of
many, and of myself also.*

Romans 16:1-2

By faith the harlot Rahab perished not with them that believed not, when she had received the spies with peace.

Hebrews 11:31

And Isaac brought her into his mother Sarah's tent, and took Rebekah, and she became his wife; and he loved her: and Isaac was comforted after his mother's death.

Genesis 24:67

CALL HER BLESSED

A woman waits for me, she contains all, nothing is lacking.

Walt Whitman

A*nd all thy children shall be taught of the* LORD; *and great shall be the peace of thy children.*

Isaiah 54:13

CALL HER BLESSED

. . .Sarah shall her name be. And I will bless her, and give thee a son also of her . . . . she shall be a mother of nations; kings of people shall be of her.

Genesis 17:15b-16

Women *wish to be loved without a why or a wherefore; not because they are pretty or good, or well-bred, or graceful, or intelligent, but because they are themselves.*

Henri Frédéric Amiel

CALL HER BLESSED

H ow *many loved your moments of glad*
   grace,
And loved your beauty with love false or true,
But one man loved the pilgrim soul in you,
And loved the sorrows of your changing face.

William Butler Yeats

H*ide not your talents, they for use were
made,*
What's a Sun-Dial in the Shade?

Benjamin Franklin

Greet Priscilla and Aquila, my fellow workers
in Christ Jesus. They risked their lives for me.
Not only I but all the churches of the Gentiles
are grateful to them.

Romans 16:3 (NIV)

Better by far you should forget and smile
Than that you should remember and be sad.

Christina Georgina Rossetti

CALL HER BLESSED

Begin at the beginning . . . and go on till you come to the end: then stop.

Lewis Carroll
(Charles Lutwidge Dodgson)

Alas! the love of Women! it is known
To be a lovely and a fearful thing.

*George Noel Gordon,
Lord Byron*

I *like not only to be loved, but also to be told*
that I am loved.

George Eliot
(Marian Evans Cross)

$\mathbb{A}$n ideal wife is any woman who has an ideal husband.

Booth Tarkington

*O*h, how hard it is to find
The one just suited to our mind!

Thomas Campbell

Life *is made up of sobs, sniffles, and smiles,*
with sniffles predominating.

O. Henry

CALL HER
BLESSED

As one whom his mother comforteth, so will
I comfort you . . . .

Isaiah 66:13

105

'Tain't *worthwhile to wear a day all out before it comes.*

Sarah Orne Jewett

"...*If everybody minded their own business*," *said the Duchess in a hoarse growl, "the world would go round a deal faster than it does.*"

Lewis Carroll
(Charles Lutwidge Dodgson)

H*e maketh the barren woman to keep house, and to be a joyful mother of children. Praise ye the LORD.*

Psalm 113:9

A *woman when she is in travail hath sorrow, because her hour is come: but as soon as she is delivered of the child she remembereth no more the anguish, for joy that a man is born into the world.*

John 16:21

109

And *they blessed Rebekah, and said unto her, Thou art our sister, be thou the mother of thousands of millions, and let thy seed possess the gate of those which hate them.*

Genesis 24:60

CALL HER
BLESSED

G*od hath taken away my reproach.*

RACHEL
Genesis 30:23

The house is old, the trees are bare,
Moonless above bends twilight's dome;
But what on earth is half so dear,
So longed for, as the hearth of home?

Emily Brontë

CALL HER
BLESSED

I *love it, I love it; and who shall dare
To chide me for loving that old armchair?*

Eliza Cook

hen Miriam the prophetess, Aaron's sister, took a tambourine in her hand, and all the women followed her, with tambourines and dancing.

Exodus 15:20 (NIV)

CALL HER BLESSED

Safe upon the solid rock the ugly houses stand:
Come and see my shining palace built upon the
sand!

Edna St. Vincent Millay

T*hose who are really in earnest must be willing to be anything or nothing in the world's estimation.*

Susan Brownell Anthony

CALL HER BLESSED

The inhabitants of the villages ceased, they ceased in Israel, until I Deborah arose, that I arose a mother in Israel.

DEBORAH
Judges 5:7

For *this child I prayed; . . . therefore also I have lent him to the* LORD; *as long as he liveth he shall be lent to the* LORD.

HANNAH
1 Samuel 1:27-28

$\mathbb{B}$*ehold the handmaid of the Lord, be it unto me according to thy word.*

MARY
Luke 1:38

My daughter, shall I not seek rest for thee, that it may be well with thee?

NAOMI
Ruth 3:1

CALL HER BLESSED

*T*hen cried a wise woman out of the city, . . .
I am one of them that are peaceable and faithful in Israel: thou seekest to destroy a city and
a mother in Israel: why wilt thou swallow up
the inheritance of the LORD?

2 Samuel 20:16,19

A *woman's advice has little value, but he who won't take it is a fool.*

Miguel de Cervantes

Beauty is in the eye of the beholder.

Margaret Wolfe Hungerford

$\mathbb{P}$*laying Shakespeare is very tiring. You never get to sit down unless you're a King.*

Josephine Hull

CALL HER
BLESSED

I*n spite of illness . . . one can remain alive past the usual date of disintegration if one is unafraid of change, insatiable in intellectual curiosity, interested in big things, and happy in small ways.*

Edith Wharton

CALL HER
BLESSED

S*he had a sister called Mary, who sat at the Lord's feet listening to what he said. But Martha was distracted by all the preparations that had to be made.*

Luke 10:39-40a (NIV)

CALL HER
BLESSED

. . . Lydia, a seller of purple, . . . whose heart the Lord opened, . . . attended unto the things which were spoken of Paul.

Acts 16:14

I *drag a boat over the ocean*
with a solid rope.
Will God hear?
Will He take me all the way?

Lal Ded

CALL HER
BLESSED

And a woman was there who had been subject to bleeding for twelve years, but no one could heal her. She came up behind him [Jesus] and touched the edge of his cloak, and immediately her bleeding stopped.

Luke 8:43-44 (NIV)

And Adam called his wife's name Eve; because she was the mother of all living.

Genesis 3:20

130

Mother is the name for God in the lips and
hearts of little children.

William Makepeace Thackeray

131

My salad days,
When I was green in judgment.

William Shakespeare

As *a jewel of gold in a swine's snout, so is a fair woman which is without discretion.*

Proverbs 11:22

So *let all thine enemies perish, O* LORD: *but let them that love him be as the sun when he goeth forth in his might. . . .*

DEBORAH
Judges 5:31

Because I was impatient, would not wait,
And thrust my willful hand across Thy threads,
And marred the pattern drawn out for my life,
O Lord, I do repent.

Sarah Williams

I *started with this idea in my head, "There's two things I've got a right to . . . death or liberty."*

Harriet Tubman

Mine eyes have seen the glory of the coming
of the Lord;
*He is trampling out the vintage where the grapes
of wrath are stored.*

Julia Ward Howe

The Mother weeps
At that white funeral of the single life,
Her maiden daughter's marriage; and her tears
Are half of pleasure, half of pain.

Alfred, Lord Tennyson

Go *not empty unto thy mother in law.*

Ruth 3:17

I*t is not our exalted feelings, it is our senti-
ments that build the necessary home.*

Elizabeth Bowen

F*or there is no friend like a sister*
In calm or stormy weather.

Christina Georgina Rossetti

$\mathbb{W}$*hether you are dealing with an animal or a child, to convince is to weaken.*

Colette

Ne one worth possessing
Can be quite possessed.

Sara Teasdale

W*hat poor astronomers are they that
Take women's eyes for stars!*

John Dowland

CALL HER
BLESSED

Beauty — *be not caused — It Is —*
Chase it, and it ceases—
Chase it not, and it abides.

Emily Dickinson

M*inds that have nothing to confer
Find little to perceive.*

William Wordsworth

CALL HER
BLESSED

I *regret the trifling narrow contracted education of the females of my own country.*

Abigail Adams
(1778)

CALL HER
BLESSED

I *too am a rare*
Pattern. As I wander down
The garden paths.

Amy Lowell

CALL HER
BLESSED

Put on with speed your woodland dress,
And bring no book; for this one day
We'll give to idleness.

William Wordsworth
(to his sister Dorothy)

"*Believe in the Lord Jesus, and you will be saved — you and your household.*"

Acts 16:31 (NIV)

Most women turn to salt . . . looking back.

Unknown

I *asked him not whence he was, neither told me his name: but he said unto me, Behold, thou shalt conceive, and bear a son . . . .*

SAMSON'S MOTHER
Judges 13:6-7

The soul can split the sky in two,
And let the face of God shine through.

Edna St. Vincent Millay

Actually, the original meaning of "lady" was "bread kneader," and if the dictionary adds, "See dough," it refers, we add sternly, to bread only.

Cleveland Amory

CALL HER BLESSED

To tell a woman everything she may not do
is to tell her what she can do.

Spanish proverb

 CALL HER
BLESSED

T*here is nothing new except that which has become antiquated.*

Mlle Bertin
(milliner to Marie Antoinette)